# HUSBANDS & WIVES

## God's Design for the Family

### BOOK 1

NAVPRESS

A MINISTRY OF THE NAVIGATORS
P.O. Box 6000, Colorado Springs, Colorado 80934

The Navigators is an international, evangelical Christian
organization. Jesus Christ gave
his followers the Great Commission to go and make disciples
(Matthew 28:19). The aim of The
Navigators is to help fulfill that
commission by multiplying
laborers for Christ in every
nation.

NavPress is the publishing
ministry of The Navigators.
NavPress publications are tools to
help Christians grow. Although
publications alone cannot make
disciples or change lives, they can
help believers learn biblical disci-
pleship, and apply what they learn
to their lives and ministries.

Sixth printing, 1984

Scripture quotations are from the
*Holy Bible: New International
Version* (NIV), © 1978 by the
International Bible Society. Used
by permission of Zondervan Bible
Publishers.

Printed in the United States of
    America

# CONTENTS

# IN RECOGNITION

These staff members of The Navigators made the major contribution to the prayerful and thoughtful preparation of *God's Design for the Family:* Rod Beidler, Bruce Das, Ray Hoo, Doug Prensner, Ed Reis, Gene Soderberg, and Bob Sparks. The aim of the series has been to provide married couples with biblical principles and patterns that lead to dynamic family growth in love, and to harmony in their relationships with God and their families.

In addition, appreciation is due to the wives of the staff members, who provided help and ideas as the project developed; to other Navigator staff members who participated in various stages of planning and preparing the series; and to a large number of staff, pastors, and lay men and women who field-tested the manuscripts.

# BEFORE YOU BEGIN

These studies are written for use by married couples, or by singles planning to be married. Both partners should answer the questions separately, and then discuss them with each other. You will gain even more benefit by meeting regularly with other couples after all of you have answered the questions. The recommended pace is one chapter per week, with a group discussion time for each chapter. Group discussion guidelines for all the chapters are included in this book, beginning on page 83.

Each chapter includes application questions and suggested family project ideas to help you apply to your family life the things you are learning in your study. Before deciding on each application, remember to pray about it. God knows the needs in your life which He wants you to work on now. Stay in communication with Him as you plan, and be confident that He will lead you. Pray also for insight and strength in putting your applications into practice.

## CHAPTER 1

# SELF-IMAGE

WHO are you? Your concept of yourself affects how you think, feel, look, and act. It also affects your relationships to God, your mate, and your children, as well as to others. When your self-concept is balanced and scripturally based, you will reap the benefits in every aspect of your life, including your marriage.

## GOD'S PLAN FOR YOU

Because God controls the circumstances of our lives, and because He is loving, we can be confident of His good plans for us. We see this demonstrated throughout Scripture.

1. Read John 10:10. Why did Jesus say He had come to us?

_____

_____

_____

_____

_____

2. In Psalm 138:8, how did David express his confidence regarding God's involvement in his life?

_____

_____

_____

3. Read Jeremiah 29:11. While Israel was in captivity in Babylon, how did God describe the plans He had for them?

_____

_____

_____

4. What confidence did Paul express in Philippians 1:6?

_____

_____

_____

5. According to Isaiah 43:7, what was God's reason for creating those who are called by His name?

_____

_____

_____

6. Read Ephesians 2:10. What does this verse tell you about (1) your worth in God's eyes and (2) your purpose in living?

_____

_____

_____

_____

_____

# RELATING
# TO OTHERS

None of us was created to exist alone. As believers in Christ, we all have a vital place in His Church: "You are the body of Christ, and each one of you is a part of it" (1 Corinthians 12:27). Therefore, the way we view and conduct our relationships with others is a crucial aspect in forming our self-image.

7. Study Galatians 5:13-14. What to you is the personal significance of this passage?

_____

_____

_____

_____

_____

_____

_____

8. Read Ephesians 5:22-24. How do you think a healthy self-image would help a wife fulfill these responsibilities?

_____

_____

_____

_____

_____

_____

11

9. Read Ephesians 5:28-29. How do you think a healthy self-image would help a husband in carrying out these responsibilities?

_____

_____

_____

_____

_____

_____

---

### RESULTS OF A WRONG SELF-IMAGE

1. Husband with an inflated self-image: He may be an unreasonable, harsh, unloving leader, making it difficult for his wife to submit, and unwilling to take suggestions from her.
2. Husband with a poor self-image: He may have the attitude, "I can't do anything right. No one could like me." He may be hesitant about providing leadership and love in his marriage.
3. Wife with an inflated self-image: She may not want to submit to her husband's leadership because she views submission as "lowering" herself, or thinks, "I can do just as well as he can."
4. Wife with a poor self-image: Lacking a realistic understanding of her abilities and strengths, she may be unable to accept sincere compliments.
5. When either a husband or wife has a weak self-concept, poor communication can result. He or she may be reluctant to express thoughts and opinions because "they're not worthwhile." Therefore, neither mate is able to really know the other, and they cannot discern each other's needs.

## ACCEPTING YOURSELF

10. Read Galatians 6:4-5. With whom are we *not* to compare ourselves?

_____

11. Read 1 Peter 1:15-16. Who *does* qualify as a standard by which we can measure ourselves?

_____

12. What purpose for evaluating ourselves did Paul give in 2 Corinthians 13:5?

_____

_____

_____

13. Our self-image is often influenced by physical problems, flaws, weaknesses, or hardships in our lives. Paul spoke of a "thorn in my flesh" which tormented him, and which he asked God three times to remove. Read God's answer and Paul's response in 2 Corinthians 12:9-10. What reason did God give for not granting Paul's request?

_____

_____

_____

_____

How did this influence Paul's attitude toward other negative circumstances? (verse 10)

_____

_____

_____

_____

14. Write down either a physical characteristic or
    something from your past that you dislike and
    consider a disadvantage, weakness, handicap,
    flaw, or problem.

    _____

    _____

    How do you think God can use this for your good?

    _____

    _____

    _____

    _____

    _____

    _____

## MAINTAINING
## A HEALTHY
## SELF-IMAGE

Your self-image has been affected by many in-
fluences: your temperament, abilities, and physique;
your parents, family, friends, and teachers; and the
unique experiences of your life. You may be unaware
of how much these have influenced your thinking
about yourself. But as a believer in Christ in posses-
sion of His Spirit and His Word, you can now take
positive steps to maintain a healthy self-image.

15. For each of the following passages, state the
    truths they express about you; then tell how you
    believe each truth should affect your attitudes or
    actions. Such attitudes as trust or self-acceptance,
    or an action such as thanking God in prayer, may
    be appropriate.

Example: Romans 8:28-29
Truth about adverse things that happen to me:

God will work for my good in everything
that happens to me, as I love Him.

Attitude or action:

I must trust God during difficult circumstances. I should not complain about
them (as I did about the hail that
damaged our garden last week. That
was wrong.)

Psalm 139:13-16
Truth about the way I am made:

Attitude or action:

15

Philippians 4:11-13
Truth about my abilities:

_____

_____

_____

_____

_____

Attitude or action:

_____

_____

_____

_____

1 Samuel 16:7
Truth about the way God evaluates me:

_____

_____

_____

_____

_____

Attitude or action:

_____

_____

_____

_____

Matthew 10:29-31
Truth about my value and what God knows about
me:

_____

_____

_____

_____

_____

_____

Attitude or action:

_____

_____

_____

Romans 12:4-8
Truth about my usefulness in the Body of
Christ:

_____

_____

_____

_____

_____

Attitude or action:

_____

_____

_____

_____

1 Corinthians 6:19-20
Truth about my body and appearance:

_____

_____

_____

_____

_____

_____

Attitude or action:

_____

_____

_____

_____

_____

16. Read Romans 12:3. How are we to think of
ourselves?

_____

_____

_____

_____

17. Look again at Romans 12:4-8. List some of your
strengths, abilities, and personal assets, then
immediately thank God for these.

_____

_____

_____

_____

_____

_____

_____

Ask your mate to confirm or add to your list.

18. What would you consider to be some of your undesirable character traits?

_____

_____

_____

Undesirable traits are often simply distorted strengths. For example, a miserly person may be basically thrifty, but carries this quality to an extreme. The chart below shows a few of these relationships between traits. The traits listed in the outer columns are the "extremes" of the qualities listed as desirable traits. In the inner columns, each line represents more or less opposite qualities. A miserly person could thus learn how to practice more generosity, and still be a thrifty person, but not miserly.

| DISTORTED TRAITS | DESIRABLE TRAITS | | DISTORTED TRAITS |
|---|---|---|---|
| Miserly | Thrifty | Generous | Financially irresponsible |
| Overbearing | Enthusiastic | Reserved | Withdrawn |
| Cold, unfeeling | Objective | Subjective | Overly emotional |
| Inflexible | Disciplined | Spontaneous | Slipshod |

19. Using the concept illustrated by the chart on page 19, and with your mate's assistance, tell what desirable traits you think underlie each of the undesirable traits you listed in Question 18.

_____

_____

_____

_____

_____

20. List some positive traits you possess that are different from those of your mate. Choose one of these and write how that difference can be used to advantage in your marriage.

_____

_____

_____

_____

_____

_____

_____

_____

21. Write a love note to your spouse and include a list of all the things you like about her or him.

22. If there is something about yourself or your past which has caused you resentment, bitterness, a lack of trust, or other wrong attitudes, write it down on the next page; then immediately confess your wrong attitude to God.

_____

_____

_____

_____

State the truth about this experience as you believe God sees it now.

_____

_____

_____

_____

How can you apply what you have learned to your life? (Cooperate with God; try to think how He may be using this to mold your life and character, and work with Him on it.)

_____

_____

_____

_____

_____

_____

Thank God for what He has done so far and will continue to do in this area of your life.

## SUMMARY

23. What are some major lessons you learned from this chapter? (List on the next page.)

21

_____

_____

_____

_____

_____

_____

_____

_____

_____

_____

## SUGGESTED FAMILY PROJECTS

(These projects, and those listed at the end of later chapters, can be a valuable exercise for practicing the scriptural principles you have studied in this chapter. As you read the instructions for the projects, think of creative ways to make them meaningful and enjoyable for each member of your family. Plan to include every child who is old enough to enjoy the time with you. If your children are older, allow time for deeper discussion of thoughts and questions they may have, and let them help you plan the project.)

a. In a time together, have each family member write down as many positive things as he can think of about the others. Then read your lists, and pray together to thank God for the way He has made each of you a unique, gifted, worthwhile individual.

b. Write letters to God thanking Him for all the things you appreciate about what He has done for each of you. Especially thank Him for how these things help you have a healthy, biblical self-image.

## CHAPTER 2

# COMMUNICATION

GOOD communication between a husband and wife will result in deeper enjoyment of each other, an ability to solve conflicts, and a greater understanding of each other's responsibilities.

## THE
## BIBLICAL
## VIEW

1. How would you define *communication?*

_____

_____

_____

_____

_____

2. What guidelines for biblical communication do you see in Ephesians 4:15?

_____

_____

_____

3. What reason for speaking truthfully is stated in Ephesians 4:25?

_____

_____

_____

_____

4. How do you think the teaching about anger in Ephesians 4:26-27 relates to communication?

_____

_____

_____

_____

_____

_____

5. What purposes for communication are described in Ephesians 4:29?

_____

_____

_____

_____

_____

6. What result of honest, wholesome communication is described in 1 Peter 3:10?

_____

_____

_____

7. According to Luke 6:45, what major factor determines the quality of our speech?

_____

_____

8. What do these passages say about the listening aspect of communication?

Proverbs 18:13_____

_____

_____

Proverbs 19:20_____

_____

_____

James 1:19_____

_____

_____

Listening involves paying close attention to what is said and accepting it as another person's thoughts or feelings, right or wrong, without condemnation. If you have really listened, you should be able to restate accurately both the content and the feeling of a message. You are not listening if you are thinking about what to say when the other person stops talking.

9. Correct timing and the right choice of words can greatly help our communication. Write in your own words the principles contained in these verses:

Proverbs 10:32 _____

_____

_____

Proverbs 15:23 _____

_____

_____

Proverbs 15:28 _____

_____

_____

Proverbs 29:20 _____

_____

_____

Colossians 4:6 _____

_____

_____

10. Good communication includes knowing when *not* to talk. List the principles from these verses:

Proverbs 10:19 _____

_____

_____

_____

Proverbs 11:13_____

_____

_____

_____

Proverbs 13:3_____

_____

_____

_____

Proverbs 17:27_____

_____

_____

_____

James 1:26_____

_____

_____

_____

11. Match the following statements with the
Scriptures that teach them.

___It's foolish to be angry.    a. Proverbs 17:9
___It's no fun to live with an   b. Proverbs 21:9
    argumentative person.   c. Proverbs 25:12
___Forgive one another;     d. Ecclesiastes 7:9
    don't keep bringing up
    past offenses.
___Wise reproof is valuable
    and should be listened to.

12. Read the following descriptions of five levels of
communication. Place a check mark by the
description of the deepest level of communication
occurring in your marriage in a typical week.

27

☐ Cliches, casual conversation. ("Hi, how are you?" "Fine.")

☐ Reporting of facts. ("The paper boy is late again.")

☐ Ideas and judgments. ("I think every man should learn how to change a diaper." "I don't agree.")

☐ Feelings and emotions. ("I like to sit by the fireplace on a snowy, dreary day like this." "So do I. It makes me feel secure and warm inside.")

☐ Open, honest sharing on a deep, personal level. ("I don't think I've been leading properly in our home. Could we talk about it? I'd like to know your thoughts." "Yes, please tell me what you've been thinking.")

Write down an example of what you discussed at your deepest level.

_____

_____

_____

_____

_____

_____

13. List any area in which you think deeper communication with your spouse is needed.

_____

_____

_____

_____

What could you do or say to achieve deeper communication in this area?

_____

_____

_____

_____

14. Indicate the type of words or speech described in each of these verses from Proverbs, and the effect this type of speech has:

| DESCRIPTION | EFFECT |
|---|---|

Proverbs 11:9

_____

_____

_____

_____

Proverbs 12:18

_____

_____

_____

_____

Proverbs 12:25

_____

_____

_____

_____

29

# Proverbs 15:1

_____

_____

_____

_____

# Proverbs 16:21

_____

_____

_____

_____

# Proverbs 16:24

_____

_____

_____

_____

# Proverbs 18:6

_____

_____

_____

_____

# Proverbs 26:28

_____

_____

_____

_____

## IMPROVING COMMUNICATION

15. Check any statements below which express problems on *your* part in your husband-wife communication.

☐ I can't seem to find the right words to express what I want to say.

☐ I'm afraid that exposing myself will result in rejection.

☐ I'm not convinced it will help any to try to talk.

☐ I often don't talk because I'm afraid my opinion is wrong.

☐ I'm too angry to talk.

☐ Speaking up will only make things worse.

☐ I talk too much and don't give my mate a chance to speak.

☐ I lack good communication with God.

☐ I try to hide the truth.

☐ My speech is often defensive.

☐ I frequently bring up his or her past failures.

☐ My actions don't match what I say.

☐ I don't really listen.

☐ I try to repay anger with anger or insult with insult.

☐ I tease my mate too much.

Choose any of the statements you checked, and write on the next page what steps you will take to deal with the problem.

31

_____
_____
_____
_____

| WAYS TO IMPROVE COMMUNICATION |
|---|

1. Don't assume you know—ask.
2. Provide an open, permissive, accepting atmosphere.
3. Use compliments freely.
4. Pray for each other, and together.
5. Be willing to disagree, but in a gentle way.
6. Concentrate on being a good listener.
7. Build up your mate's self-esteem.
8. Seek more to understand than to be understood. ("I'm not sure I understand. Could you repeat that?")
9. When you are wrong or have sinned against your mate, admit it and ask forgiveness. Put it into words: "Will you forgive me?" and "Yes, I forgive you."

## APPLICATION

16. Prayerfully review your answers in this chapter, and summarize the major lessons you learned.

_____
_____
_____
_____
_____
_____

17. Carry out at least one of these two items:
Ask God to show you what steps He wants you to
take to improve your communication. Write your
plan here.

_____

_____

_____

_____

_____

Make a written agreement with your mate to communicate more effectively, listing specific things
you have learned.

_____

_____

_____

_____

_____

_____

_____

## SUGGESTED
## FAMILY
## PROJECT

Take each child individually for a walk or go out for
a snack or a meal, and concentrate on *listening* to
the child. Ask him questions based on what he is talking about, instead of subjects you think of. Let it be
a time of natural, unhindered expression for him.
(Each parent could do this, at different times.)

## CHAPTER 3

# LOVE AND LOVING

LOVE is not a unique aspect of marriage—marriage is a unique aspect of love. Marriage does nothing to guarantee love—but love does everything to guarantee a marriage. A marriage relationship not founded on scriptural love is limited. But when Christ's love is preeminent in a marriage, lasting joy and peace will be experienced.

In the Scriptures we can explore what love is, and how it can be applied in a Christian marriage.

## GOD'S LOVE

1. What do these verses in 1 John 4 say about love?

Verse 8 _____

_____

_____

Verse 12 _____

_____

_____

Verse 19 _____

_____

_____

2. God *is* love, and His love is the model for our love. In the following verses we can observe specific characteristics of God that reveal His love. Some of these are listed in the middle column. Look up the verses to see how these characteristics are mentioned, and then tell how God manifests these characteristics to us.

|  | CHARAC-TERISTIC | MANIFESTATION TOWARD US |
|---|---|---|
| Exodus 34:6-7 | Compassion | |
| | Graciousness | |
| | Patience | |
| | Forgiveness | |
| | Justice | |
| Deuteronomy 33:12 | Protection | |
| Psalm 89:32-33 | Faithfulness | |

| Jeremiah 31:3 | Steadfastness | _____ |
| | | _____ |
| | | _____ |
| John 3:16 | Generosity | _____ |
| | | _____ |
| | | _____ |
| Romans 5:8 | Absoluteness | _____ |
| | | _____ |

3. According to Romans 8:38-39, what can change God's love for us?

_____

4. Knowing the characteristics of God as they are revealed in Scripture can help us develop an accurate concept of God's love, and allow us to respond properly to Him. From Psalm 63:3, how did David respond to God's love?

_____

## LOVE IN MARRIAGE

5. Read Jesus' teaching on love in John 13:34-35, then check the answer or answers below which best complete this statement: A Christian husband and wife must love each other . . .

☐ because their marriage will be immeasurably more successful if they do.

☐ with the same unselfish love with which Christ loves them.

☐ because a loving Christian couple is a distinctive testimony to the world.

37

6. Read Matthew 22:34-40. What is the second greatest commandment?

_____

_____

How do you think this commandment applies to marriage?

_____

_____

_____

_____

7. Read Colossians 3:14. What is the source of unity in a marriage relationship?

_____

Do you think this love comes naturally? Why or why not? (You may want to refer to Galatians 5:22.)

_____

_____

_____

What is a probable cause when disunity disrupts your relationship with your mate?

_____

_____

_____

What should you do about it?

_____

_____

_____

_____

8. What truth and application regarding love's place in your marriage can you derive from 1 Corinthians 8:1 and Ephesians 4:29?

| TRUTH | APPLICATION |
|-------|-------------|
|       |             |
|       |             |
|       |             |
|       |             |
|       |             |

9. Read 1 Peter 3:8-9, and list the things that should characterize our relationships.

10. Explain how the principle in 1 John 4:18 can promote the honest expression of attitudes and feelings between marriage partners.

## THE LOVING HUSBAND

11. (For husbands) When you say to your wife, "I love you," what are you trying to tell her?

_____

_____

_____

_____

_____

12. Review God's command to husbands in Ephesians 5:25-30. In light of this passage, check the statements below which correctly describe how a husband should demonstrate his love for his wife.

☐ By asserting his God-ordained authority over her.

☐ By always taking the initiative to restore a strained or broken relationship, no matter who is at fault.

☐ By sacrificially spending himself for her welfare.

☐ By loving her affectionately and physically.

☐ By making her spiritual welfare the first priority of your relationship.

☐ By encouraging and assisting her to become all that God wants her to be.

☐ By having her remain in her place in the home.

13. Look again at Ephesians 5:28-29, and write a statement of how you believe a husband can provide this kind of care for his wife.

_____

_____

_____

_____

14. On the basis of 1 Peter 3:7, evaluate these statements and record your thoughts:

Christianity advocates that men give women a place of honor. The ways in which women differ from men is a cause for men to respect them, not to degrade them.

_____

_____

_____

_____

_____

If a man is experiencing difficulty in his relationship with God, he would be wise to consider whether he is giving his wife the honor she deserves.

_____

_____

_____

_____

15. Attitudes are communicated verbally and nonverbally in marriage. Match the references below with the statement that describes the correct attitude a loving husband should communicate to his wife.

___"There's no way I could ever get along without you."

___"Since you came into my life, my relationship with the Lord has grown."

___"You are the greatest!"

___"I have perfect confidence that you can do anything."

a. Proverbs 18:22

b. Proverbs 31:10-11

c. Proverbs 31:28-29

d. Genesis 2:18

41

## THE LOVING WIFE

16. (For wives) Briefly describe what you mean when you tell your husband you love him.

_____

_____

_____

_____

_____

17. When the Bible commands the husband to love his wife (as in Ephesians 5:25), the Greek word used for love is *agapao*. The *agapao* type of love "is not an impulse from the feelings, it does not always run with the natural inclinations, nor does it spend itself upon those for whom some affinity is discovered. Love seeks the welfare of all."*

When the wife, on the other hand, is taught to love her husband (Titus 2:4), the Greek word for love is *phileo*. "*Phileo* is to be distinguished from *agapao* in this, that *phileo* more nearly represents tender affection."**

What significance do you see in the different types of love to be given by the husband and the wife in these two instances?

_____

_____

_____

18. Read Titus 2:4-5. Paul's teaching here includes some of the proper responsibilities associated with a woman's love (*phileo*) for her husband. What are they?

*W.E. Vine, *An Expository Dictionary of New Testament Words* (London: Oliphants, Ltd., 1940), volume III, page 21.
**Vine, *New Testament Words*, volume III, page 21.

_____

_____

_____

_____

19. According to Proverbs 31:12-27, what are some
additional ways in which a wife can communicate
her love for her husband?

_____

_____

_____

_____

_____

_____

_____

_____

20. What negative quality showing a lack of love is
mentioned in Proverbs 27:15?

_____

_____

21. Read 1 Peter 3:1-6. What do you think Peter
meant by emphasizing the wife's development of
her "inner self, the unfading beauty of a gentle
and quiet spirit"?

_____

_____

_____

How do you think these qualities are to be developed?

_____

_____

_____

_____

## APPLICATION

22. Review your answers in this chapter, and find a particular truth about love that needs to be applied or reinforced in your life. List the truth here, and describe how you will apply it.

_____

_____

_____

_____

_____

_____

_____

_____

## SUGGESTED FAMILY PROJECT

Ask each other the following question: "What is it that I do for you that makes you feel loved?" To answer, take a piece of paper and write "I feel loved when you . . ." at the top of the page, and then list as many answers to the question as possible. (For example: "I feel loved when you bring me a cup of coffee while I'm balancing the checkbook.") This could be done with husbands and wives only, or with children as well.

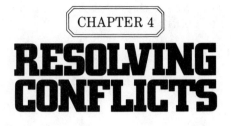

CHAPTER 4

# RESOLVING CONFLICTS

CONFLICT is normal and natural in the development of relationships—especially in marriage, where two unique individuals enter into an intimate union. In marriage, conflicts arise because husbands and wives have different opinions, values, philosophies, and methods. Conflict in marriage may be developmental, or it may be devastating—depending on how it is handled. The art of resolving conflicts is a key to keeping a marriage healthy. It is a measure of maturity, and part of the lifelong process of "two becoming one."

## SOURCES OF CONFLICT

The husband and wife are each unique. They have different responses and reactions. One may be more logical and objective, the other more emotional and impulsive. One may be active and aggressive, while the other is more sensitive and emotionally stable. Whatever their differences, the husband and wife must work together to understand and support one another.

1. Besides natural differences between people, the Scriptures address other factors that can cause

45

conflict. Read the verses below, and tell what each one teaches about the correct way to deal with sources of conflict.

Differences in the strength of our faith—Romans 14:1

_____

_____

_____

_____

Failings by those who are weak—Romans 15:1-2

_____

_____

_____

_____

_____

Tendency to be ambitious and conceited— Philippians 2:3-4

_____

_____

_____

_____

_____

2. What potential sources of conflict can you identify from these verses?

Jeremiah 17:9_____

_____

_____

_____

_____

Romans 7:18-19_____

_____

_____

_____

_____

_____

3. Summarize how James described the source of conflicts in James 4:1-3.

_____

_____

_____

_____

_____

4. Read 1 Corinthians 3:1-3. What reasons did Paul give for the jealousy and quarreling among the Christians in Corinth?

_____

_____

_____

_____

5. Evaluate the list on page 48 of factors which can help cause disunity in marriage. Rate each item to indicate how significant these are in your own marriage:

    N - Never produces a conflict

    S - Sometimes produces a conflict

    O - Often results in a conflict

| CIRCUMSTANCES | BEHAVIOR CHARACTERISTICS |
|---|---|
| ___ Fatigue | ___ Unrealistic expectations |
| ___ Unfulfilled needs | ___ Unwillingness to communicate |
| ___ Financial difficulties | ___ Sarcasm or demeaning remarks |
| ___ Busy schedule | ___ Making false assumptions |
| ___ Family background | ___ Jumping to conclusions |
| ___ Relatives | ___ Inflexibility |
| ___ Lack of fellowship with God | ___ Irritating habits |
| | ___ Tactlessness |
| ___ _____ | ___ Nagging |
| ___ _____ | ___ _____ |

Discuss your answers with your spouse. Conflicts can often be resolved simply by determining what is creating them and taking steps to eliminate their causes, or at least lessening their influence.

6. Read Matthew 7:1-5, and choose the best answer or answers below.

According to this passage, Jesus taught that:

☐ Conflict in interpersonal relationships is inevitable.

☐ Conflict should be avoided by simply over-looking other people's faults and weaknesses.

☐ Conflict usually intensifies when one fails to recognize and correct his own faults.

☐ Conflict can be avoided by not judging other people for their faults and weaknesses.

7. How could you apply Galatians 3:26-28 to conflict in marriage?

_____

_____

_____

_____

_____

_____

_____

_____

_____

_____

_____

8. Circle your response to the following statements.

a. Conflicts are always caused by the differences between husbands and wives. *Agree / Disagree*

b. Conflict is an important element in the personal growth of a husband and wife. *Agree / Disagree*

c. Conflicts are not always accompanied by arguments. *Agree / Disagree*

d. Unresolved conflicts usually become "problems" in a marriage. *Agree / Disagree*

e. Each time an old conflict resurfaces without a resolution, the "problem" becomes more acute. *Agree / Disagree*

## RESOLVING CONFLICTS

9. Select one of the following verbal expressions as an example of the way you responded to a recent conflict in your marriage.

☐ "It's not important enough to bring up and risk ruining our relationship, so I'll forget it."

☐ "There's no way to resolve this conflict, so why try?"

49

☐ "Let's talk about it. Christ can help us
resolve our conflict."

☐ "Some day I may say something about it,
but today I'll just wait and see if it might
resolve itself. There are other things we
can talk about."

What were the advantages and disadvantages of
this approach?

_____

_____

_____

_____

_____

10. Compare Matthew 5:23-24 and Matthew 18:15-18.
How are the principles in these two passages fun-
damentally the same?

_____

_____

_____

_____

In what respects do they differ?

_____

_____

_____

_____

11. What are the implications of not resolving a conflict, as presented in Matthew 5:23-24?

_____

_____

_____

12. In Matthew 6:14-15, what importance does Jesus place on the resolution of conflicts?

_____

_____

_____

If it is not resolved, what effect does a conflict have on our relationship with God?

_____

_____

_____

13. In your own words, briefly summarize the principles from the passages in Questions 10-12.

_____

_____

_____

_____

_____

_____

14. Based on a study of 1 Corinthians 13:6, how could love resolve a conflict?

_____

_____

_____

_____

_____

15. Read 1 Samuel 15:1-15. How did Saul first respond when Samuel confronted him with his sin?

_____

_____

_____

_____

16. Read 2 Samuel 12:1-13. When David was confronted with his sin, how did his response differ from Saul's?

_____

_____

_____

_____

17. When the Holy Spirit uses your mate to convict you with the truth of your sin in a conflict, what response do you believe is most pleasing to God?

_____

_____

_____

_____

_____

How do you normally respond when confronted with such a situation?

_____

_____

_____

_____

18. What counsel does Jesus give in Luke 17:3-4 regarding total reconciliation?

_____

_____

_____

_____

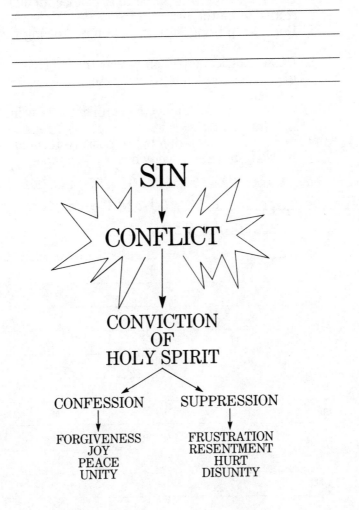

SIN

CONFLICT

CONVICTION
OF
HOLY SPIRIT

CONFESSION                SUPPRESSION

FORGIVENESS              FRUSTRATION
JOY                      RESENTMENT
PEACE                    HURT
UNITY                    DISUNITY

53

| FOUR "DON'TS" IN RESOLVING CONFLICTS |
|---|
| 1. Don't wait for your mate to apologize; don't refuse to be the first to give in. |
| 2. Don't keep bringing it up and not allowing the conflict to end. |
| 3. Don't attack the person rather than the conflict (which amounts to character assassination). |
| 4. Don't walk out, killing the conflict in its prime. |

19. Rewrite the above "don'ts" in positive form as they relate to you, as shown in the example:

a. *Even if both of us are wrong I should apologize immediately when I'm aware of my sin.*

b. _____

_____

_____

_____

c. _____

_____

_____

_____

d. _____

_____

_____

_____

## APPLICATION

20. Summarize the lessons you have learned from this chapter.

_____

_____

_____

_____

_____

_____

_____

_____

_____

_____

21. If any conflict exists in your marriage, write out what you are going to do in the coming week about settling it, and include the scriptural principles on which you will base your actions.

_____

_____

_____

_____

_____

_____

_____

_____

**SUGGESTED
FAMILY
PROJECT**

Discuss with your spouse these additional suggestions for resolving conflicts:

55

a. Sit down so you face each other.
b. If the discussion becomes more heated, lower your voices. Avoid shouting.
c. Work at clearly defining the issue so both of you understand what the conflict is about.
d. Seek counsel from someone you respect and trust (such as your pastor or a close friend) if you cannot resolve the conflict yourselves. Another person often can be more objective.
e. Make resolving the conflict a priority. Don't let anything interfere with resolving it, even if it means canceling a planned appointment or activity.

## CHAPTER 5

# SEXUAL INTIMACY

## INFLUENCES ON SEXUAL ATTITUDES

UNDERSTANDING common philosophies regarding the physical relationship between a man and a woman, and how they may have affected your thinking, can serve as a useful background for studying biblical principles in this area. Two of these philosophies, in their extremes, can be described in this way:*

*Eroticism.* According to erotic philosophy, there are no moral or spiritual absolutes. The flesh is of greatest consequence, and the highest good is to be found in satisfying one's own physical appetites.

*Asceticism.* The ascetic philosophy maintains that anything which satisfies the flesh is evil. That which is physical cannot be enjoyable. Sensual desire and sexual expression are therefore evil and destitute of spiritual value. Sex is considered a purely utilitarian function for the procreation of the human race.

The following four questions may help you understand your own and your mate's background.

*Summarized from *Sexual Happiness in Marriage* by Herbert Miles (Grand Rapids, Michigan: Zondervan Publishing House, 1967), page 24.

1. As you were growing up, what was the prevailing philosophy in society regarding sex? (Circle the appropriate answer.)

| Very Ascetic | Mildly Ascetic | Mildly Erotic | Very Erotic |

2. Circle the category which describes your own family's attitude toward discussing sex as you were growing up.

| Closed | Discreet | Open | Indiscreet |

3. Which, if either, of the ascetic or erotic philosophies has had the greatest influence on your present feelings about sex?

_____

4. Without asking your mate, which of the two philosophies do you think has had the greatest influence on his or her present feelings about sex?

_____

After you have answered the first four questions, plan to discuss them with your mate.

5. Read 1 Peter 4:1-5. Which statement below best expresses the attitude God expects Christians to have toward the erotic philosophy of sex?

☐ Eroticism is essential if maximum sexual satisfaction is to be achieved within the Christian marriage.

☐ Eroticism is contrary to the will of God.

☐ If eroticism is helpful in your marriage relationship and meets the needs of both partners, then it is acceptable.

6. Read Colossians 2:20-23. How is the ascetic philosophy expressed in this passage?

_____

_____

What is the source of the rules stated in
verse 21?

_____

_____

_____

How effective are these rules?

_____

_____

_____

7. Read 1 Timothy 4:1-3. Which of these statements
summarize how God describes the proponents of
ascetic values?

☐ They are earnestly seeking the will of God.

☐ They have been led astray.

☐ They are hypocrites with seared
consciences.

☐ Because of their discipline, they will be
able to stand strongly in the face of
temptation.

8. According to 1 Timothy 4:3-5, what should be the
Christian's attitude toward the pleasurable things
of which the ascetic would deprive himself?

_____

_____

_____

_____

_____

_____

9. How would you summarize God's attitude toward
these two philosophies regarding sex?

59

_____

_____

_____

_____

_____

_____

## GOD'S PURPOSE
## FOR SEXUALITY

10. The Bible states that man was created in God's own image. Read Genesis 1:27, and list another distinct characteristic in the way God created humanity.

_____

11. From the passages below, list God's purposes in creating man distinctly male and woman distinctly female.

Genesis 2:24_____

_____

_____

Genesis 4:1_____

_____

_____

Proverbs 5:18-19_____

_____

_____

12. Compare verses 27 and 31 of Genesis 1. After creating man and woman, what did God say?

_____

13. From Genesis 2:25, how did the man and woman feel about the way God had created them?

_____

_____

Read Genesis 3:6-10. How did the man and woman's attitude change?

_____

_____

_____

From the context of these two passages, what caused their change in attitude?

_____

_____

_____

14. Would you say your feelings regarding your own sexuality are more characteristic of Genesis 2:25 or Genesis 3:7? Why?

_____

_____

_____

_____

15. Read Song of Songs (Song of Solomon) 5:10-16 and 7:1-9, then select the best answer or answers to this question: How should a husband and wife feel about the characteristics of each other that arouse sensual excitement?

☐ Although the characteristics may be greatly appreciated, expressing those feelings is in bad taste.

61

☐ They should feel the freedom to express exactly how they feel about what arouses them.

☐ Such feelings are unspiritual in nature and should be avoided by modesty in dress and appearance.

## GOD'S DESIGN FOR SEXUAL EXPRESSION

16. Read 1 Corinthians 6:9-10. What forms of sexual expression are not acceptable to God?

_____

_____

_____

_____

17. From Hebrews 13:4, describe God's attitude concerning sexual relationships being exclusively within the context of marriage.

_____

_____

_____

18. Compare the lovemaking experiences found in these passages, and record your thoughts concerning each:

Song of Songs 4:1—5:1_____

_____

_____

_____

_____

Proverbs 7:1-23 _____

_____

_____

_____

_____

_____

19. What do the passages below say about sexual experiences?

Proverbs 5:15-19 _____

_____

_____

Proverbs 6:32-33 _____

_____

_____

20. Read 1 Corinthians 7:3-5. What attitude should a husband and wife have toward each other's sexual desires?

_____

_____

_____

_____

21. As applied to marriage, the principles found in Philippians 2:3-4 can reveal sources of difficulty in the sexual relationship. Check the statement or statements in the following list which describe a difficulty that could be overcome by practicing the principles of this passage.

☐ Failure to consider one another's emotional and sexual needs.

☐ An overemphasis on the importance of one's own sexual needs.

☐ Considering one's partner as a sex object rather than a person.

22. From Philippians 2:5-8, how is Jesus Christ the model for marriage partners in fulfilling each other's needs?

_____

_____

_____

_____

_____

_____

_____

## APPLICATION

23. Review your answers in this chapter, and find a truth you need to apply or reinforce in your life. How do you intend to apply it to your present situation?

_____

_____

_____

_____

_____

## SUGGESTED FAMILY PROJECT

Plan to discuss your sexual relationship with your spouse to increase your enjoyment of your relationship by gaining a better understanding of each other's desires. You may want to read together a good book on the sexual relationship (such as one of those listed on page 95).

## CHAPTER 6

# RESPONSIBILITIES

GOD wants your marriage to be a picture of His love for the Church, which he calls the Bride of Christ and the Body of Christ. To accomplish this, He has given special responsibilities to both partners in a marriage. Some of these responsibilities are unique to either the husband or the wife, while others are shared by both.

## JOINT RESPONSIBILITIES

A husband and wife who are Christians share some obligations to each other that are inherent in their relationship with Christ. These responsibilities would be theirs whether or not they were married, but carry greater significance because of their union with each other.

1. What command regarding our relationships is given in Ephesians 5:21?

   _____

   _____

   _____

   _____

What are some examples of how the guidelines in Ephesians 5:21 should be applied to a marital relationship?

_____

_____

_____

_____

_____

_____

2. Choose one or two of the qualities mentioned in each of these passages, and tell how they should be applied in your marriage:

Galatians 5:22-23_____

_____

_____

_____

_____

Colossians 3:12-14_____

_____

_____

_____

_____

3. Read through all of the following statements and place a circle around the answer which represents your opinion. Then read the Bible verse given next to each statement, and indicate with a square the position supported by that verse.

A = Agree       D = Disagree

a. I usually should not tell my mate that he (or she) has hurt me. (Ephesians 4:15)      A    D

b. I should point out sin in my mate's life.
(Galatians 6:1) A D

c. When something is troubling my mate, I should let him (her) work through it alone.
(Galatians 6:2) A D

d. I should not admit any of the sins I am struggling with to my mate because he (she) may lose respect for me. (James 5:16) A D

e. Both the husband and the wife are to grow spiritually. (2 Peter 3:18) A D

Set aside a time this week to discuss your answers with your spouse.

4. Summarize in your own words how the following passages relate to your marriage.

Romans 15:5-6 _____

_____

_____

1 Peter 4:8 _____

_____

_____

5. From 1 Thessalonians 5:14-15, list any principles that could help you relate better to your husband or wife, and tell how they could be applied.

_____

_____

_____

_____

69

# THE HUSBAND'S RESPONSIBILITIES

6. Read Ephesians 5:23. What unique position does the husband have in marriage? What does this mean to you?

_____

_____

7. Read 1 Corinthians 11:3 and Philippians 2:5-6, then check the statements below which are true.

☐ God is the head over Christ.

☐ God is superior to Christ.

☐ The husband is the head over the wife.

☐ The husband is superior to the wife.

☐ God and Christ are equal.

☐ The husband and the wife are equal.

8. Read 1 Peter 5:1-3, and check the correct statements.

Biblical leadership is characterized by:

☐ Operating according to God's plan.

☐ Motivation for gain by the leader.

☐ Willingness to lead.

☐ Eagerness to serve.

☐ Being domineering over those in the leader's charge.

☐ Being an example.

9. Review Ephesians 5:25-33. What is the pattern for how a man should love his wife?

_____

_____

10. To get a better idea of how husbands are to love
their wives, let us consider how Christ loves us as
believers. Summarize what the following passages
tell us about Christ's love, and describe how this
could be reflected in a husband's relationship with
his wife.

| HOW CHRIST LOVES US | APPLICATION TO THE HUSBAND-WIFE RELATIONSHIP |
|---|---|
| Psalm 23:4 | |
| | |
| Matthew 11:28-30 | |
| | |
| John 10:11 | |
| | |
| John 13:12-15 | |
| | |

71

John 14:1-2

_____

_____

_____

_____

John 17:20

_____

_____

_____

_____

Romans 8:38-39

_____

_____

_____

_____

11. What are some situations from your experience or observation in which it can be difficult for a husband to love or lead his wife?

_____

_____

_____

_____

_____

_____

12. Number the different items you listed in Question 11; then match them with the following guidelines which could help the husband in each situation.

(Write the numbers in the blank spaces.) More than one guideline may seem appropriate to you for some situations.

___ Pray for her. ("Always keep on praying for all the saints"—Ephesians 6:18.)

___ Tactfully communicate with her, explaining why he is having difficulty, and asking for her help and cooperation. ("Love must be sincere" —Romans 12:9.)

___ Forgive her. ("Forgive as the Lord forgave you"—Colossians 3:13.)

___ Initiate love toward her, just as God has done. ("We love because He first loved us"—1 John 4:19.)

___ Don't hold her wrong attitudes or actions against her (Love "keeps no record of wrongs"—1 Corinthians 13:5), but be patient with her.

___ Seek to gain a better understanding of her, such as by getting advice and insight from others. ("Listen to advice and accept instruction, and in the end you will be wise"— Proverbs 19:20.)

___ Other: _____

_____

13. Write in your own words the principles taught in 1 Peter 3:7.

_____

_____

_____

_____

14. (For husbands) Check the reasons why you have sometimes hesitated to lead your wife:

    ☐ It takes more effort to lead than I am willing to expend.

    ☐ I didn't understand that God holds me responsible for leading.

    ☐ My wife often has not followed me when I have tried to lead.

    ☐ I was afraid of failure.

    ☐ My wife has belittled my decisions or suggestions in the past.

    ☐ Other: _____

    _____

    Set aside a time this week to discuss your answers with your wife.

15. Look again at Ephesians 5:28-29 and 5:33. How can these verses help you understand how a husband should love his wife?

    _____

    _____

    _____

    _____

    _____

    _____

16. (For husbands) Prayerfully review your answers about the husband's responsibilities, then write down one thing you believe you should do to become a better husband.

    (For wives) Prayerfully review what you have learned about the husband's responsibilities, then write down one thing you can do to encourage and help your husband carry out his responsibilities.

_____

_____

_____

_____

## THE WIFE'S RESPONSIBILITIES

When God created woman, He said, "It is not good for the man to be alone. I will make a helper suitable for him" (Genesis 2:18). God designed women to be capable of being a complementary partner to man—just what the man needs—although He did not set this as a limit to a woman's potential.

This role is not demeaning, nor does it imply any loss of identity for the wife. In fact, the Hebrew word that is translated *helper* in Genesis 2:18 is used often to describe God as being man's help (as in Psalm 33:20—"He is our *help* and our shield"). Being a wife is a dignified, responsible, and honorable position.

17. What does Proverbs 12:4 teach about wives?

_____

_____

_____

18. How are the wife's responsibilities described in Ephesians 5:22-24 and 5:33?

_____

_____

_____

75

According to these verses, in what situations is a wife to submit to her husband?

_____

_____

19. From Ephesians 5:22-23, can you discover an explanation for why God designed the husband-wife relationship in this way?

_____

_____

_____

_____

Just as God is the head of Christ, and yet Christ and God are equals, so it is with husband and wife. The responsibility of submitting does *not* mean the wife is inferior to her husband.

20. With help from other resources, such as a dictionary, how would you define *submission*?

_____

_____

_____

_____

21. Study the description of Jesus' submission in Philippians 2:5-9. Which of the following statements are true?

☐ The *attitude* of submission is important.

☐ Jesus did not hold on to His "rights."

☐ Jesus humbled Himself to submit; no one forced Him to do so.

76

☐ Because He submitted to God, Jesus lost His importance and His identity.

☐ Jesus' submission resulted in great glory and honor for Him.

22. With Ephesians 5:24 in mind—"As the church submits to Christ, so also wives should submit to their husbands"—let us consider how the Church submits to Christ, and how you think this can be applied by a wife. Use the passages listed below to complete the chart.

| HOW THE CHURCH SUBMITS TO CHRIST | APPLICATION TO THE HUSBAND-WIFE RELATIONSHIP |
| --- | --- |

Matthew 11:28-30

_____

_____

_____

_____

_____

John 10:14

_____

_____

_____

John 10:27

_____

_____

_____

_____

John 12:26

_____
_____
_____
_____

Philippians 4:6

_____
_____
_____
_____

1 Peter 4:12-13

_____
_____
_____
_____

2 Peter 3:18

_____
_____
_____
_____

23. What are some situations from your experience or observation in which it can be difficult for a wife to respect or submit to her husband?

_____
_____
_____
_____

24. Number the different items you listed in Question 23, then match them with the guidelines listed below which could help the wife in each situation.

___ Pray for him.

___ Tactfully communicate to him her thoughts on the situation. ("Through patience a ruler can be persuaded"—Proverbs 25:15.)

___ Forgive him.

___ Let him know she trusts his judgment and will obey and support him in whatever he decides. ("Obey your leaders . . . so that their work will be a joy, not a burden" —Hebrews 13:17.)

___ Seek to gain a better understanding of him, such as by getting advice and insight from others.

___ Love him. ("As I have loved you, so you must love one another"—John 13:34.)

___ Obey him and trust God to use the situation for their good. ("We know that in all things God works for the good of those who love Him, who have been called according to His purpose"—Romans 8:28.)

___ Other: _____

_____

25. (For wives) Check the reasons why you have sometimes hesitated to submit to and respect your husband's leadership.

___ My husband has not satisfactorily demonstrated that he loves me and wants my best.

___ I didn't realize that I am responsible to God for submitting to my husband, even though I am not responsible for the outcome of his decisions.

___ My husband's wishes conflict with my own.
___ I want something my husband is not interested in or opposes.
___ My husband wants me to violate God's moral law.
___ Other: _____

_____

Set aside a time this week to discuss your answers with your husband.

26. (For wives) Prayerfully review your answers about the wife's responsibilities, then write down one thing you believe you should do to become a better wife.

(For husbands) Prayerfully review this section on the wife's responsibilities, then write down one thing you can do to encourage and help your wife carry them out.

_____

_____

_____

_____

_____

## SUMMARY

27. What are some major lessons you learned from this chapter?

_____

_____

_____

_____

_____

# SUGGESTED FAMILY PROJECT

At a time when you are all together, have each family member tell what his most important responsibilities are in your family. Also, consider sharing with your children how you plan to encourage each other in your marriage relationship as an example to them of helping each other in practical ways.

# GUIDELINES FOR GROUP DISCUSSION

Discussing this book in a group—such as a Sunday school class or a Bible study group—will allow greater understanding of the scriptural principles you study. The format for this is simple: The group members first answer the questions to a chapter individually at home, and then discuss their findings with each other when they meet together, which is usually once a week.

If you are the discussion leader for such a group, the material on the following pages will help you guide the group in an edifying time of fellowship centered on God's Word.

## BEFORE THE DISCUSSION

As the group leader, your most important preparation for each session is prayer. You will want to make your prayer requests personal, of course, but here are some suggestions:

• Pray that everyone in the group will complete the chapter preparation, and will attend this week's discussion. Ask God to allow each of them to feel the freedom to honestly share his thoughts, and to make a significant contribution to the discussion.

• Ask God to give each of you new understanding and practical applications from the Scriptures as you talk. Pray that the unique needs of each person will be met in this way.

• Pray that you, as the leader, will know the Holy Spirit's guidance in exercising patience, acceptance, sensitivity, and wisdom. Pray for an atmosphere of genuine love in the group, with each member being honestly open to learning and change.

• Pray that as a result of your study and discussion, all of you will obey the Lord more closely and will more clearly demonstrate Christ's presence in your families.

After prayer, the next most important aspect of your preparation is to be thoroughly familiar with the chapter you're discussing. Make sure you have answered all the questions and have read the leader's material for that chapter.

## GETTING UNDER WAY

When your group is together, work toward having a relaxed and open atmosphere. This may not come quickly, so be especially friendly at first, and communicate to the group that all of you are learning together.

As the leader, take charge in an inoffensive way. The group is looking to you for leadership and you should provide it.

You may want to experiment with various methods for discussing the study material. One simple approach is to discuss it question by question. You can go around the group in order, with the first person giving his answer to Question 1 (followed by a little discussion), the second person answering Question 2, and so on. Or, anyone in the group could answer each question as you come to it (the leader saying something such as "Who would like to take Question 5 for us?"). The question-by-question approach can be a good way to get young Christians started in Bible study discussion. The obvious structure gives them a sense of confidence, and they can see where the discussion is going.

Another method is to lead with a section-by-section

approach. This can provide more spontaneity. Start by asking the group for its impressions of the first section in the chapter you are studying (something like, "What impressed you most from this first section on prayer?"). Remember to direct your question to the entire group, rather than to a certain person.

Someone will then give an answer, probably by referring to a specific question in that section. You can have others share their answers, and then, to discuss the question more thoroughly, ask a thought-provoking question about this topic which you have made up beforehand. Later you'll begin this procedure again with the next section.

The key to a deeper, more interesting and helpful discussion is having good questions prepared. These should challenge the group to look more closely at the subject and Scripture passage you are discussing.

This leader's material includes suggested discussion questions for each chapter in this book. However, you will probably want to write some of your own as well, so make a list before each group meeting. Write as many as you can think of. Having a good supply to choose from will help you quickly launch the discussion, and keep it going in the right direction.

These guidelines will also help:

*Asking questions*

1. Make sure your questions are conversational.
2. Don't be afraid of silence after asking a question. Give everyone time to think.
3. Ask only one question at a time.
4. Don't ask questions which can be answered yes or no. This hinders discussion. Try beginning all your questions with "who," "what," "where," "when," "why," or "how."
5. A "What do you think?" question can help keep the discussion from seeming pressured or unnatural, since there is no such thing as a wrong answer to such a question. The person answering has freedom to simply give his viewpoint.

85

*Other discussion*
1. Remember that the Scriptures are the source of truth. Often you may want to look up together and read aloud the verses listed for the study questions as you discuss your answers.
2. Summarize frequently. Help the group see the direction of the discussion.
3. Allow time for adequate discussion on the application questions in each chapter. Your goal in Bible study is not, of course, to have something to discuss, but to change your lives.
4. Allow adequate discussion also of the suggested family projects. Talk about how these can be adapted and implemented by everyone in the group.

*General reminders*
1. Your own attitude is a key factor in the group's enthusiasm. Develop a genuine interest in each person's remarks, and expect to learn from them.
2. Concentrate on developing acceptance and concern in the group. Avoid a businesslike atmosphere.
3. Participate in the discussion as a member of the group. Don't be either a lecturer or a silent observer.
4. You may want to begin each session by reviewing memorized Scripture, and then discussing progress made in the previous week on applications and family projects.
5. Your total discussion time should probably not exceed ninety minutes, and one hour might be best. Start and end on time. Remember, too, to close in group prayer.

You'll want to review these lists often.

## AFTER
## THE DISCUSSION

Use these self-evaluation questions after each session to help you improve your leadership the next time:
1. Did you discuss the major points in the chapter?
2. Did you have enough prepared questions to properly guide the discussion?

3. Did you know your material thoroughly enough to have freedom in leading?
4. Did you keep the discussion from wandering?
5. Did everyone participate in the discussion?
6. Was the discussion practical?
7. Did you begin and end on time?

# Chapter 1

## SELF-IMAGE

| OVERVIEW | OBJECTIVE |
|---|---|
| a. God's plan for you<br>b. Relating to others<br>c. Accepting yourself<br>d. Maintaining a healthy self-image<br>e. Summary | For each participant to maintain a healthy, biblical self-image by learning how God views us and how we should regard ourselves. |

For this session, and in later weeks, you may want to read the chapter objective and overview aloud to the group. This can help them see the overall focus of the chapter as they begin their discussion. You may also want to review these at the end of the discussion.

These questions from the study may promote the best discussion in your group as you share with each other your answers to them:

1, 5, 6, 7, 8, 9, 11, 12, 13, 15, 16, 17, 20, and 23.

Other suggestions:

• Have some of the group members read aloud the material on "Results of a Wrong Self-Image" (page 12).

• For each passage in Question 15, have one or two group members give their answers, followed by discussion in the group.

It is often helpful to have someone read aloud a key passage pertaining to the chapter topic. A key passage for this chapter is Romans 12:4-8.

Each chapter in the study material includes application questions. These are designed to help a person apply a biblical truth to his life in a practical way. Since the written answers for these questions are personal, group members need to have the freedom *not* to share their answers when you are discussing these questions. On the other hand, don't skip over the questions entirely, since the most beneficial discussion you can have is about how the Scriptures affect your day-to-day life.

A good way to stimulate discussion on an application question is to say something like, "Would any of you like to share with us your answers to Question 14?" or, "What did you learn about yourself (or your family) from Question 14?"

(In Chapter 1, Questions 14, 17, 21, and 22 are application questions.)

Remember to discuss also the suggested family projects. You may want someone to read aloud the instructions. Then discuss how the projects can be used and adapted most effectively in each family represented in your group.

## FOR FURTHER DISCUSSION

These questions can help you stimulate further discussion on some of the questions in this chapter:

For *Question 1:* How would you compare what Jesus says here to what people generally think of today as a good life?

*Question 2:* How is God's purpose for us an expression of His love?

*Question 5:* How does God's creation give Him glory?

*Question 6:* How would these truths relate to our ability to carry out God's will?

*Question 7:* Do you think loving others is a necessary requirement for having a good self-image?

*Questions 8-9:* How would you summarize the benefits of a healthy self-image for husbands and wives?

*Question 12:* What do you think is the proper way to examine or test ourselves?
*Question 13:* What would cause your family to be content with weaknesses, hardships, and difficulties?
*Question 16:* How does faith relate to our self-image?

## Chapter 2

## COMMUNICATION

| OVERVIEW | OBJECTIVE |
|---|---|
| a. The biblical view<br>b. Improving communication<br>c. Application | To understand the biblical principles of communication, and to begin applying them in our marriages—becoming better listeners and establishing a deeper level of communication with each other. |

These questions from the study may promote the best discussion in your group:
1, 4, 8, 9, 11, and 16.
The application questions are 13, 15, and 17. Remember also to discuss the suggested family project.

You can launch a discussion of Questions 12 and 13 simply by asking, "Would any of you like to summarize some things you learned in Questions 12 and 13?"

You may want to have the group read aloud and discuss the material on "Ways to Improve Communication" (page 32).

At one or two points in the discussion, you may find it appropriate to have a few moments of group prayer about a specific aspect of the study, such as becoming a better listener and a more effective communicator in your marriages.

## FOR FURTHER DISCUSSION

For *Questions 2-3:* Why is truth a key ingredient in effective communication?

*Question 4:* What are the dangers of prolonged anger?

*Question 5:* What is an example of unwholesome speech? What is an example of speech which builds others up?

*Question 7:* How do we store up either good or evil in our hearts?

*Question 8:* How can we improve our ability to listen to what others say?

*Question 9: (Colossians 4:6):* What do you think it means for our conversation to be "full of grace" and "seasoned with salt"?

*Question 11 (Proverbs 17:9):* What is the best way to "cover over an offense"?

## Chapter 3

## LOVE AND LOVING

| OVERVIEW | OBJECTIVE |
|---|---|
| a. God's love<br>b. Love in marriage<br>c. The loving husband<br>d. The loving wife<br>e. Application | To understand the nature of God's love, and how a couple can follow His loving example with practical expressions of their love for one another. |

These questions from the study may promote the best discussion in your group:
5, 6, 7, 10, 11, 13, 14, 16, 19, and 21.

The application questions are 7 and 22. Remember also to discuss the suggested family project.

A good passage to have someone read aloud is 1 Corinthians 13:4-7, perhaps from *The Living Bible* or the J. B. Phillips translation.

## FOR FURTHER DISCUSSION

For *Questions 1-2:* How is it a help in your marriage to know that God is love?

*Question 3:* Do you ever *feel* as though God has stopped loving you?
Why is it wrong to feel this way?

*Question 7:* How does love promote unity?
What other aids to unity in marriage can you think of?

*Question 9:* Are there times when it is okay *not* to have harmony in our relationships?

*Question 10:* What kind of fears can repress love in a marriage relationship?

*Question 12:* Why do you think God has given husbands such a high standard to follow in loving their wives?

*Question 14:* What are some practical ways husbands can demonstrate respect for their wives?

*Question 15:* How often should a husband express his love for his wife?

*Question 18:* How do these things demonstrate love?

## Chapter 4

## RESOLVING CONFLICTS

| OVERVIEW | OBJECTIVE |
|---|---|
| a. Sources of conflict<br>b. Resolving conflicts<br>c. Application | To analyze the usual sources of conflicts in our marriages, and to learn how to effectively resolve conflicts by applying scriptural principles. |

91

These questions may promote the best discussion in your group:
2, 5, 6, 7, 8, 9, 13, 14, 17, 18, 19, and 20.
Question 21 is an application question.

The material on "Four "Don'ts" in Resolving Conflicts" (page 54) and in the suggested family project can be read aloud and discussed in your group.

Especially if it seems obvious that some group members are experiencing difficulty in resolving marital conflicts, you could stress in your discussion that conflicts are normal in human relationships, that solving them requires commitment and mutual effort, and that biblical reconciliation is of crucial importance.

## FOR FURTHER DISCUSSION

For *Questions 1-4:* The Scriptures mention many potential sources of conflict. Which do you feel are the most common sources of conflict today?

*Question 1:* Give examples of how each of these can cause conflicts: differences in the strength of our faith; failings by those who are weak; and the tendency to be ambitious and conceited.

*Question 3:* How can selfishness be controlled?

*Question 6:* What are some ways in which we tend to show our judgment of others?

*Question 7:* Who is the key person in resolving conflicts?

*Question 9:* Often it is difficult for a husband and wife to begin a discussion about a conflict they are having. What ideas can you suggest for making it easier to begin such a conversation?

*Questions 10-13:* Why is our relationship with God affected so much by our relationships with each other?

*Question 14:* How are we sometimes tempted to "delight in evil" instead of "rejoicing with the truth"?

*Question 15:* How are we tempted to rationalize our sins?

*Question 18:* Should we be unlimited in our forgiveness? Why or why not?

# Chapter 5

## SEXUAL INTIMACY

| OVERVIEW | OBJECTIVE |
|---|---|
| a. Influences on sexual attitudes<br>b. God's purpose for sexuality<br>c. God's design for sexual expression<br>d. Application | To become aware of how our backgrounds have shaped our sexual perspectives, and to understand God's perspective and design for sexual intimacy in marriage. |

These questions may promote the best discussion in your group:
   3, 5, 6, 9, 11, 13, 15, 17, 21, and 22.
Question 23 is an application question.

## FOR FURTHER DISCUSSION

For *Question 8:* Why is thanksgiving important in our attitude toward everything God has created and given us?

*Question 11:* Do these biblical purposes still hold true today?

*Question 13 (Genesis 2:25):* What would enable couples today to enjoy the same kind of relationship that Adam and Eve at first experienced in the Garden of Eden?

*(Genesis 3:6-10):* How does sin affect your views of your own manhood or womanhood?

*Question 16:* How should this teaching influence our attitude toward persons who practice or approve of these sins?

*Question 17:* What could happen if this teaching is not followed?

## Chapter 6

# RESPONSIBILITIES

| OVERVIEW | OBJECTIVE |
|---|---|
| a. Joint responsibilities<br>b. The husband's responsibilities<br>c. The wife's responsibilities<br>d. Summary | To understand our responsibilities to God and to our marriage partner, and to take practical steps to carry out these responsibilities. |

A good passage to have someone read aloud (perhaps in a modern paraphrase) is Ephesians 5:22-33.

These questions may promote the best discussion in your group:

1, 3, 4, 7, 8, 9, 10, 13, 18, 19, 20, 21, 22, and 27.

Application questions include 14, 16, 25, and 26.

## FOR FURTHER DISCUSSION

For *Question 4 (Romans 15:5-6):* How does our unity result in glory to God?

*(1 Peter 4:8):* How does love cover over sins?

*Question 5:* What are some times when a husband and wife need encouragement from each other?

*Question 10:* How would you explain the impact a husband can have on his family if he follows these biblical guidelines?

*Question 18:* What are examples of some ways in which wives should submit to their husbands?

*Question 21:* What do you think motivated Jesus to submit in this way to God and to man?

*Question 22:* How would you explain the impact a wife can have on her family if she follows these biblical guidelines?

# SUGGESTED READING

Augsburger, David. *Caring Enough to Confront.* Glendale, California: Gospel Light—Regal Books, 1973.

Evans, Louis H. *Your Marriage—Duel or Duet?* Old Tappan, New Jersey: Fleming H. Revell, 1962.

Howe, Reuel L. *The Miracle of Dialogue.* New York: Seabury Press, 1963.

LaHaye, Tim and Beverly. *The Act of Marriage.* Grand Rapids, Michigan: Zondervan Publishing House, 1976.

Mayhall, Jack and Carole. *Marriage Takes More Than Love.* NavPress, 1978.

Osborne, Cecil. *The Art of Understanding Your Mate.* Grand Rapids, Michigan: Zondervan Publishing House, 1974.

Petersen, J. Allan, with Smith, Elven and Joyce. *Two Become One.* Wheaton, Illinois: Tyndale House, 1973.

Powell, John. *Why Am I Afraid to Tell You Who I Am?* Niles, Illinois: Argus Communications, 1969.

Shedd, Charlie. *Talk to Me!* New York: Doubleday, 1975.

Tournier, Paul. *To Understand Each Other.* Atlanta: John Knox Press, 1967.

Trobisch, Ingrid. *The Joy of Being a Woman.* New York: Harper and Row, 1975.

Trobisch, Walter. *I Married You.* New York: Harper and Row, 1971.

Wheat, Ed and Gaye. *Intended for Pleasure.* Old Tappan, New Jersey: Fleming H. Revell, 1977.

Wright, H. Norman. *Communication: Key to Your Marriage.* Glendale, California: Gospel Light—Regal Books, 1974.